How to Sail Around the World Part-Time

by

Linus Wilson

Oxriver Publishing

Lafayette, Louisiana, U.S.A.

a division of

Vermilion Advisory Services

ISBN-13: 978-0692641224

ISBN-10: 069264122X

Dedication

To all my friends and newsletter subscribers who made the first book of this unknown author a #1 bestseller in Kindle sailing narratives,

and to my parents who have supported me in everything I have done.

You can join the adventures of the *Slow Boat* crew. If you want to know more about future books and my family's travels, get free chapters or books, boat repair tips, and news of discounts, subscribe to my free newsletter at www.slowboatsailing.com.

Contents

1.   My Failure

It was a successful cruise. The boat was not wrecked, not badly at least. Our cruise of the Bahamas, chronicled in *Slow Boat to the Bahamas,* was never really delayed. We never hit bad weather—at least while my wife was aboard! That was both due to luck and prudent planning. I don't think that my wife, Janna, my 4-year-old daughter Sophie, and I were underway in more than 20 knots of wind. That was more than we could say of our adventures closer to home. On that Bahamas cruise, I did all the maintenance and repairs for the diesel inboard and dinghy outboards, and they kept pushing us forward. Nevertheless, ideas for future extended cruises were shot down by Janna quickly and forcefully.

In June 2015, I bought "the Bible" for world cruisers, Jimmy Cornell's *World Cruising Routes,* and carefully studied the World ARC routes. On a scrap piece of paper, I scratched out a rough schedule. From December 2016 to June 2017 we could move the boat from New Orleans to Grenada and sail the length of the Caribbean to Panama. We then could transit the Panama Canal. Next, free from North Atlantic hurricane season, we could sail to French Polynesia and then to Fiji where I had seen the *Wizard's Eye*, a sailboat which is the subject of a YouTube series, hauled out.

By that time, it would be November 2017, and we would both need jobs to occupy us while waiting out the South Pacific Cyclone season. I probably could get an internship in the private sector, government, or a visiting teaching position with a university. (I'm a finance professor.) Janna, the M.D., could get a *locum tenens* or a temporary position with a practice while another doctor was on leave. By May 2018, we could be underway again and in Darwin, Australia by November of that year. We would get six month jobs waiting out the November to April cyclone season in the South Indian Ocean. In May 2019, we would sail across the Indian Ocean to Madagascar and South Africa. Because there is no hurricane activity in the South Atlantic Ocean, we could press on to Brazil, and then the eastern Caribbean, and arrive in Miami by May 2020. That was my plan for a fast, three-and-a-half-year circumnavigation.

Unfortunately, whenever I would mention my cocktail napkin planning in summer 2015 to Janna, she ran away as if I were offering her raw sewage on a platter.

"I think we could just cruise six months of the year and live on land in the U.S. for the other six months," I offered.

She replied, "I don't enjoy cruising as much as you do, and I can't really picture myself living on the boat for more than a couple of months per year. Sophie and I would miss the richness of life on land. Besides, I am deathly afraid of ocean passages."

Her response was hardly encouraging. I felt that I could justify the long absence from full-time work to employers and myself if it were for a circumnavigation. In contrast, a Caribbean cruise, the stuff of two-week charters, would be seen as just being a beach bum. I'm not saying that there is anything wrong with catching rays and enjoying life. It is just not me. I don't really like to be on beaches or in the sunshine. I prefer doing math problems to laying on a beach towel. I would just see two years of a Bahamas or eastern Caribbean cruise as not worth giving up a job I loved. Unfortunately, the Bahamas or eastern Caribbean cruising was all the adventure Janna would consider on our boat.

Whenever I broached the circumnavigation plan, Janna would deflect me with, "I have no objections to you doing this without me and Sophie. I know how much you love sailing." At first I resented her answer.

"You underestimate me if you think that I would never take you up on the offer," I replied.

"I'm just saying that you can do that on your own. I'm scared of crossing the ocean," Janna said.

Necessity is the task master of all men. I really did not want to quit my job to cruise the eastern Caribbean. In my mind, going to the eastern Caribbean was mostly a way to ease Janna into more serious ocean voyaging. We had visited Antigua. We had chartered in St. Vincent and the Grenadines. Besides, the end of our circumnavigation would take us to the eastern Caribbean anyway.

The problem with my thinking about a circumnavigation was that I thought we would start in the eastern Caribbean in the first year. To cruise the eastern Caribbean, you have to cruise between December and May to avoid hurricane season. Thus, my summer breaks from teaching were useless for cruising the islands.

Nevertheless, if I skipped the eastern Caribbean and got to Panama before hurricane season, I would not have to worry about tropical storms during my summer breaks until I moved the boat over 24,000 nautical miles west around the world. By that time, I would be eligible for another sabbatical. Thus, the idea for the part-time circumnavigation was born. I had to get my *Slow Boat* to Panama. Janna promised to come with Sophie when I got there.

Figure 1: Common Western Hemisphere stops on a trade-wind circumnavigation mentioned

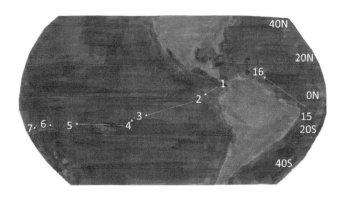

1. Panama, 2. The Galapagos, 3. The Marquesas, 4. Tahiti and Raiatea, 5. Fiji, 6. Vanuatu, 7. New Caledonia, 15. Brazil, 16. eastern Caribbean

Figure 2: Common Eastern Hemisphere stops on a trade-wind circumnavigation mentioned

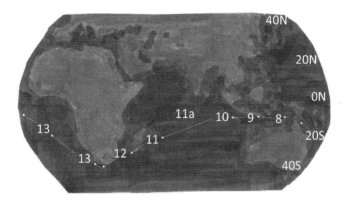

8. Darwin, Australia, 9. Bali, Indonesia, 10. Cocos Keeling, 11. Mauritius, 11a. Chagos, 12. Durbin, South Africa, 13. Cape Town, South Africa, 14. St. Helena; All the stops listed prior to the eastern Caribbean are safe from tropical storms during the Northern Hemisphere summers.

2.   Summiting Everest v. Circumnavigation

In 2013, 658 people summited Mount Everest. About half of these were local high-altitude porters commonly known as Sherpa. Most of the rest were not professional mountaineers. Instead, they were part-time enthusiasts who were guided to the top of the world for a price tag of more than $50,000. This outdoor adventure trophy included bad food, frequent dehydration, frequent headaches, starvation-like weight loss, altitude sickness, over a month in a cold, uncomfortable tents, and a one-in-ten chance of death. Since expeditions began on the world's highest peak in the 1920s through 2013, for every ten people that have summited Mt. Everest roughly one has died trying. [i] Specifically, 1.1 percent of climbers leaving Everest base camp between 1953 and 2012 have died on the attempt to climb and descend this peak.[ii]

This number may understate the risk because fatalities spiked on Everest in 2014 and 2015. In 2014, an enormous block of ice dislodged and killed 16 climbers. At least 19 climbers died in the aftermath of the Nepali earthquake of 2015.[iii] Many of those that don't die are maimed for life. Frostbite claimed fingers and toes as low atmospheric oxygen, cold temperatures, and fickle weather combined with lethal force.

To get to the top, most climbers walk next to the frozen mummies of climbers who sacrificed their lives in a vain attempt to summit and return from the deadly Himalayan peak. Nevertheless, the view from the top is often worse than what the typical commercial airplane flyer can see from the window seat of a safe, $400 flight from Indianapolis to Baltimore.

There is another outdoor adventure prize at the feet of the amateur, which involves swaying palms, days on the beach, warm water, boundless sunsets, and nights full of more stars than most readers have ever seen. This adventure involves no exhausting hikes with heavy packs, no pitching of tents, plenty of food and drink, and running (hot and cold) water. This rarer prize is the circumnavigation of the globe in a small sailboat. (I arbitrarily define small as under 70 feet long.) I will refer to sailors in small boats as cruisers. By my estimates, which I will explain subsequently, the death rate for circumnavigating the globe in a cruising sailboat is closer to 0.3 percent. This is less than the 1.1 percent for those going higher than Everest base camp. Moreover, few climbers ascend Everest on their first attempt, which may double or triple the risks. Finally, the miniscule daily circumnavigation risks are spread out over six years, not the less than six weeks it takes to summit Everest.

Three-time circumnavigator, Jimmy Cornell, the founder of the most popular around the world rally for sailboats (the World ARC) estimates that, based on yachts' checking in at key ports around the globe, about 150 to 200 sailboats complete a circumnavigation each year.[iv] Based on the

Latitude 38 "West Coast Circumnavigators' List" that I analyzed, the average boat circumnavigating for the first time has 1.9 people going around the whole way. That translates into about 280 to 380 people circumnavigating each year. That is about half as many people as climbed Mount Everest in 2013. The number of small boat circumnavigators each year is about at parity with the non-Sherpa climbers of Everest in 2013.

More potential circumnavigators die of illnesses unrelated to their sailing than drowning. Indeed, the death statistics of potential circumnavigators lost at sea in yachts is so small that there seem to be no reliable statistics on the risks of a 26,000-nautical-mile journey in a small sailboat. (A nautical mile is approximately 1.15 statute miles. One nautical mile is one minute of latitude. 60 minutes of latitude make up each degree of latitude.) Surely crossing oceans in a sailboat is dangerous, but it may be less dangerous than being a cheerleader.[v]

The World ARC circumnavigation route is roughly 25,000 nautical miles. (Participants likely rack up far more sea miles because of side trips and tacking into headwinds.) With an average pace of four miles an hour underway, the trip would take 6,250 hours. I used U.S. Coast Guard statistics to estimate the death rate per hour of sailing in 2011. That is about 0.3 percent for every 10,000 hours. Over the course of a 6,250-hour journey, it works out to a 0.2 percent chance of death while sailing.

Cruisers also spend a lot of time in their small tenders going to and from the mother ship. If they spend an hour a day in their dinghy for the 5.94 years of an average circumnavigation, this translates to a 0.1 percent chance that they will die in their dinghy over the course of the long trip. The death rate in dinghies was about 0.5 percent per 10,000 hours in 2011, but over about six years the cruiser is estimated to spend 2,167 hours in her dinghy.[vi] Over that period, certainly risks such as heart disease and cancer loom larger for cruisers older than 50 than does death associated with boating accidents. If the cruiser's boat averages over four knots for a faster trip, the calculated risk decreases because the total hours go down.

If those cruisers stop driving and riding in cars over those six years, they can reduce their chances of death in an automobile accident by 0.05 percent over that period.[vii] In 2009, the average American spent almost 1,000 hours driving in or riding in automobiles. If we subtract out the risks of going back to one's land-based, automobile-focused existence, then the typical six-year circumnavigation has a chance of death of about 0.25 percent or about 1 in 400. Another way of looking at it is that circumnavigating is about six times more dangerous than your regular commute of nearly 1,000 hours in your car per year. Per hour of activity, sailing is about 3.5 times more dangerous than riding in a car. Riding in a dinghy is about six times more dangerous per hour than riding in a car. In all three cases, only after over 10,000 hours of activity does the mortality risk surpass 0.5 percent.

On a per-hour basis, climbing on Everest is much more dangerous. I used the average times for climbs above base camp from an Everest climbing website.[viii] At a minimum, from the books and movies that I have read and seen about Everest, guided climbers try to climb to Camp 3 (8,000 meters) at least twice. The first time is to acclimatize to the altitude, and the second time is to climb the mountain. I doubled the climb times to Camp 3 to allow for descents and added 16 hours at each camp above base camp (1, 2, 3, and 4) for rest. From what I read, climbers only go to Camp 4 and the summit once a season. Thus, the average times for Camp 4 and above were recorded only once. That gives me 146 hours above base camp. Using the 1.1 percent mortality rate above base camp between 1953 and 2012, an hour above base camp on Everest is 264 times more dangerous than an hour of sailing.

Why do so many more people succeed at climbing Mount Everest than sailing around the world? My guess is that climbing Mount Everest is a part-time pursuit. It only takes about two months in the Himalayas to acclimatize and find the appropriate weather window. Many amateur climbers that survive the mountain don't succeed on their first attempt and must come for two or more expeditions. Moreover, few climbers will attempt Everest and few guides will accept clients who have not summited some other large glaciated peaks such as Denali (also known as Mount McKinley), 20,322 feet, or the "safest" 8,000+-meter peak of Cho Oyu at 26,906 feet.[ix] Multiple, multi-week expeditions are often necessary to get up these training peaks and the training peaks for Denali or Cho Oyu. Mount Rainier, 14,409 feet, and Kilimanjaro, 19,341 feet, are examples of the latter. These expeditions up "training" peaks are also dangerous, but I have not included the very large mortality risks of climbing these lesser peaks on the way to an Everest summit.

Amateur climbers can piece together vacations and short leaves of absences from their jobs to build their experience on high mountains and eventually summit the biggest mountain—if they don't die along the way. They typically have to shell out well over $100,000. My guess is that $200,000 to $300,000 is a better estimate of the outlays on the way to the top of Everest. Moreover, they must build up a high level of cardiovascular fitness, which usually far exceeds say what is necessary to complete a marathon, to trudge up fixed ropes with oxygen masks strapped to their faces. The high-altitude porters can carry most loads, but can't carry climbers up to and down from the top of the world.

In contrast, sailing around the world is assumed to be a full-time pursuit. You have to quit your job and live on a boat. That is the conventional wisdom at least. You need to cut your ties to land, house, car, and take your kids out of school, if they have not yet flown the coop. The Everest summiteers do none of this. They rarely climb the mountain with their significant other, who may not like mountain climbing as much as their spouse. In contrast, first-time circumnavigators, according to my analysis of the *Latitude 38* list, are couples at 57 percent.

If your boat is your year-round home, you will want a bigger boat than if it is simply your vacation cottage. Thus, the idea that a circumnavigation is a year-round pursuit may have prompted sailors to buy bigger (more expensive) boats than if they saw it as a part-of-the-year, second home. I looked at the first-time circumnavigators from the *Latitude 38* list to estimate the trends in boat size since 1950. My estimates say that the average circumnavigator's boat, departing in 2015, will be 49 feet long. However, many people have completed the circle in much smaller (less expensive) boats.

The cost to outfit and maintain a 49-foot boat is likely to exceed the huge sums amateur climbers shell out to eventually be guided to the top of Everest. A successful circumnavigation takes six years on average. If the crew of those boats leave the workforce for all six years, lost wages for these people probably far exceed the actual costs of outfitting, maintaining, and buying the sailboat. It seems likely that the amateur Everest climbers only loses a year or less of work to pursue their climbing dreams. This in part explains why retirees are more common than younger cruisers. If the person is retired, there are no lost wages from sailing around the world for six years.

I suspect another big reason for the low number of circumnavigations is the lack of focus. The myth is that on a circumnavigation you will "see the world." Unfortunately, there are far too many interesting stops accessible by water to see them all. If a cruiser stops everywhere, she will run out of time, money, health, or some combination of the three. Mountain climbers do not suffer from this lack of focus. Their goal is not to see every inch of the mountain. Instead, they aim for a line to the top and a line back down to base camp. Similarly, circumnavigation is a line around the world. It is not a zig-zag stopping at every interesting port in the world's oceans.

3. Geography and Tropical Storm Seasons

The standard trade-wind circumnavigation for cruisers starts and ends in the eastern Caribbean and goes through the Panama Canal, the South Pacific, north of Australia, though the South Indian Ocean to Madagascar, around South Africa, up the South Atlantic, and back to the eastern Caribbean. (See figures 1 and 2 just prior to Chapter 2.) For boats starting on the west coast of North America, if they go to the South Pacific before the eastern Caribbean, they probably complete the circumnavigation offshore along the Mexican coast. Many boats from the west coast of North America will opt to go east in the Panama Canal and explore the eastern Caribbean before crossing the Panama Canal east to west and tackling the Pacific Ocean. In that case, the eastern Caribbean will also be where they first complete their circumnavigation. For boats from Europe or the eastern coast of North

America, they will complete the circumnavigation crossing their outbound tracks in the eastern Caribbean. Boats departing from New Zealand, Australia, South Africa, and South America will likely first cross their outbound tracks near their home ports.

The increase in Somali pirate activity in the Gulf of Aden and the capture, ransom, and deaths of cruising boat crews have recently dissuaded most cruising boats from circumnavigating by way of the Mediterranean and Red Seas. The capture of the U.S.-flagged sailing vessel *S/V Quest* in 2011 and the subsequent shootings of its four crew members has stopped almost all cruising boats from transiting the Suez Canal up to the time of writing in 2016.

Even before the increase in piracy, the Suez Canal route was a difficult passage for most sailing vessels. Heavy ship traffic made it hard to keep crew rested. East to west circumnavigators faced winds, which were primarily northerly with frequent gales opposing their progress up the Red Sea. Dust storms coated their decks, hardware, and sails. Moreover, Saudi Arabia, the western shore of the Red Sea, was off-limits to cruising boats. In the film, *Beyond the West Horizon*, Eric Hiscock said of his 1952 to 1955 circumnavigation in a small yacht with his wife, "We had chosen to come not the easy way around the Cape of Good Hope but the more difficult way up the Red Sea." Once a boat made it to the Suez Canal, cruisers often complained that rampant corruption, "baksheesh", greeted them in Egypt.

The Mediterranean is on a fairly high latitude. It is cold, and the winds are not as predictable in the trade-wind belt. A boat could spend two decades exploring "the Med" as Franz Amussen has talked about in his *Sailing in the Mediterranean* podcast or sail its length it in a month. Amussen sails his boat a couple of months per year. Nevertheless, he warns gale force *Meltemi* storms are common. In their film, *Beyond the West Horizon*, Eric and Susan Hiscock said their greatest winds of the trip, 80 knots, were experienced in port on the

Greek island of Rhodes in the Mediterranean.

The region around the equator is a dead zone for tropical storms. Hurricanes and typhoons rarely get close to the equatorial latitudes referred to as the doldrums or Inter-Tropical Convergence Zone (ITCZ). The ITCZ is subject to fickle winds, frequent calms, and numerous thunder squalls. The most common circumnavigation today, starting in the eastern Caribbean, going through the Panama Canal, and sailing around South Africa, will spend most of its sea miles, 95 percent, in the ITCZ or the southern hemisphere. In this route across the ITCZ and southern hemisphere only the transits of the South Pacific or South Indian Oceans are subject to the threat of revolving tropical storms. The South Atlantic is not plagued by tropical storms, nor is Panama or the northern coast of South America.

There is a myth circulated by sailors of the "endless summer", to borrow a phrase from the title of the famous surfing film. The myth is that circumnavigators can avoid hurricane and typhoon seasons by skillfully moving around the trade-wind belt. In practice, this is not possible. What happens, in fact, is the full-time cruisers get caught in an endless washing machine. They end up repeatedly circling the same patch of stormy ocean, trying to avoid cyclone season.

For two-thirds of the sea miles, the typhoon season runs from November to April or May. The South Indian typhoon seasons run from November to April or May. Likewise, the South Pacific typhoon season runs from November to April. That means that, for prudent cruisers, large ocean passages are off the table in the majority of the circumnavigation from November to April. From roughly the Galapagos Islands about 850 miles west of Panama near the equator to Durbin, South Africa, ocean passages in November through April must be avoided. That is over 17,000 nautical miles! A cruising boat would not be able to stop for any length of time during the six months from May to October, when southern hemisphere cyclones rarely occur. Few boats or their crews are able to maintain that pace.

In practice, cruisers often spend typhoon season in the danger zone. New Zealand, Australia, Fiji, New Caledonia, the Cook Islands, and Samoa are places in the South Pacific where cruisers have been known to park their boats in the November to April. This is not much different from what boaters in the U.S. do. Many boaters risk hurricanes by parking their boats on the Gulf of Mexico and Atlantic coasts. Many boats were destroyed when Hurricane Katrina devastated eastern Louisiana and Mississippi and when Hurricane Sandy hit New York and New Jersey.

The best sailors can do is to moor, haul out, or tie up their boats well during hurricane, cyclone, and typhoon season and not be on their boats when the big one hits. My home port of New Orleans housed my sailboats from 2010 to 2016, but I did not lose sleep about dying in a hurricane because I had no intention of being on my boat when the next one hit.

With this huge expanse of desirable cruising grounds in the South Pacific, crossing in one season means that interesting stops will have to be skipped in a mad rush to get to "safe" Australia or New Zealand. A better option is to haul out the boat in Raiatea or securely tie it to a marina in Papeete, Tahiti. Go back to your job or home for between ten and six months and pick up cruising again sometime between May and September. Visit Tonga and Fiji and haul out the boat in Fiji. Again, go back to your job or home for between ten and six months and pick up cruising again sometime between May and September. Visit Vanuatu and New Caledonia, and haul out or tie up in a marina for six to 10 months while you are gone. From there, you can decide if you want to cruise Indonesia or Australia and the Great Barrier Reef.

Sure you could spend years exploring Australia full-time, as you probably could any continental sized nation such as the U.S., Russia, or China. However, few Americans sailing the South Pacific want to devote years crisscrossing the U.S. in a recreational vehicle. Why should so many potential circumnavigators feel like they must do that in Australia? Such journeys, while potentially interesting, miss the point of a circumnavigation. It is sailing a line around the world. It is not a complete exploration of every pocket of the globe. Why not buy an RV and travel across Asia! It might be fun, but it has nothing to do with sailing around the world. Sailing from New Caledonia to Darwin, Australia on the northwest coast is about 4,000 nautical miles. That is a trip that can be accomplished in two to six months.

Alternatively, the boat can be left in some other Australian port along the way, leaving the passage to Darwin and Indonesia for another season. A part-timer can park the boat in Indonesia for a season. Lombok and Bali are candidates.

The transit across the Indian Ocean to approximately Durbin, South Africa on the northeast coast of South Africa makes many potential circumnavigators sell their boats in Australia. Nevertheless, the sea miles, about 5,000, are less than the transit from Panama to Tahiti. Moreover, that ocean crossing is broken up by stopovers along the way (the Cocos Keeling, Chagos, or Mauritius) unlike the 3,000-nautical-mile trip from the Galapagos to the Marquesas in the eastern Pacific.

According to Jimmy Cornell, in 2010 826 boats made it to Tahiti, but those numbers had thinned considerably in Australia where only 450 foreign yachts checked in that year. The numbers dwindle further when one looks at the popular mid-Indian Ocean stopovers of Mauritius and Chagos. The North route around Madagascar stops at the island of Chagos and the south route around Madagascar often has boats stopping at Mauritius. There were only 104 and 125 foreign boats, respectively, checking in at Chagos and Mauritius. It would be nice to have more recent numbers because almost all potential circumnavigators are skipping the Red Sea since the murders of the crew of S/V Quest in 2011 by Somali pirates.

Madagascar is notorious for petty theft. That may deter many from leaving their boats there hauled out and unattended for six to 10 months. Leaving the boat in South Africa probably means that a part-timer will want to leave the boat in South Africa nearly a year. In the next season, the part-time circumnavigator will tackle the tricky rounding of Cape Agulhas.

This is a dangerous stretch of water with strong currents and the seemingly endless fetch of the notorious Southern Ocean. Some of the biggest waves ever recorded were around Cape Agulhas. A boat with a good engine will want to port-hop and pick its rounding window carefully. The Agulhas current runs along the east coast of South Africa. This will speed the east to west (trade wind) circumnavigators' trips, but the sailors must carefully avoid south winds, which can kick up monstrous seas. It should be treated with at least as much care as the north Atlantic's Gulf Stream current. The Agulhas current is a problem that must be managed both on the approach to South

Africa's north-east coast and on the rounding of that great cape.

If the cruiser's boat makes it to Cape Town, that is probably a good place to stop if immigration will allow it. Multi-entry visas or temporary resident permits are probably worth investigation prior to landing in South Africa. Boats will cross the South Atlantic from Cape Town on the western side of South Africa, and Jimmy Cornell argues that most will stop in St. Helena in the South Atlantic on the way to Brazil. This Atlantic crossing with the southeast trades on the stern is about 3,600 nautical miles. Once in Brazil, the part-time circumnavigator will probably want to haul out and go home before another ocean voyage or long cruise. This stretch of water has no tropical storms so the part-time circumnavigator is not limited to only May to November as she has been for the last several years since leaving Panama.

Since the path to the Caribbean goes through the fickle winds of the ITCZ, the doldrums, the cruiser may want to port-hop to keep the diesel tanks full. Going offshore certainly does not save many miles as you angle for the southeast Caribbean. Trinidad has good marine facilities and is out of the north Atlantic hurricane zone. The world cruiser may want to choose this as the next place to haul out and store her boat.

Once back in the Caribbean, the part-time circumnavigator will have to change her schedule. She can only cruise from December to May to avoid hurricane season. By this time, most boats will be very close to closing the circle on their outbound track and technically completing the circumnavigation. If they still have money and still love boating, they will want to savor the beam reach of the eastern Caribbean. Most boats from the Atlantic basin will probably want to leave the islands and be almost home before June. The west coast sailors that explore the eastern Caribbean in one season will want to sail to Panama before June and haul out there to wait out eastern Pacific hurricane season before making their way north to their home ports. The Pacific coast of

Mexico is a dangerous place to be in a boat during hurricane season.

4.   The Round-Trip Problem

In some sense, cruising permits with three-to-six-month time horizons check this temptation to linger, but many cruisers counteract this tendency by returning year after year to the same cruising grounds. Seasonal weather patterns and hurricane and typhoon seasons also push boats to not linger for the whole year. For example, my wife and I met cruisers (small sailboat owners) who had visited the Bahamas over 20 times. With over 300 islands, mostly uninhabited, they had more places to explore. Nevertheless, my personal opinion was that sampling a new cruising ground would be a more interesting experience than honing an expertise in sailing in the beautiful Bahamas.

For people cruising between Florida and the Bahamas, as Martin Lane-Smith did early on in his cruising on his sailing catamaran *Dos Gatos*[x], the round trip is not too time consuming. However, when the cyclone season port is thousands of miles of open ocean away from the desirable cruising grounds, a seasonal migration is a bigger drain on the crew's time and patience.

Pacific cruisers often rush from the eastern Caribbean to Australia or New Zealand in less than 12 months. This fast pace and heavy doses of ocean crossings in a single year can take a lot out of a boat and its crew. After years of a few thousand miles a year, Caribbean cruisers continuing on a circumnavigation jump to about 10,000 nautical miles in a single year. This is a huge increase in miles and long ocean passages. This is the prescription of the World ARC, and the experience of many cruisers crossing the Pacific after cruising the Caribbean. Martin Lane-Smith and his partner departed from Trinidad in the eastern Caribbean in November 2006 and arrived in Australia in November 2007. At the same time, this means these cruisers feel they have missed out on exploring Tonga, Fiji, and Vanuatu.

Strict limits on cruising permits in French Polynesia prevent full-time, live-aboard cruisers from lingering on its islands of the Marquesas, Tuamotus, Tahiti, and Raiatea. However, a part-time circumnavigator could leave her boat for a year in French Polynesia even if she could only stay in that country for 90 days.

The round trip to the "safe" home port on the mainland means many sea miles are over old ground. If someone is in the trade-wind belt, that often means that one part of the round trip is rough. Many Pacific cruisers leave the trade-wind destinations of Fiji, Tonga, and Vanuatu to go to "safe" New Zealand. Nevertheless, that usually means a rough passage on one leg of the roughly 1000-nautical-mile trip to or from Auckland. New Zealand is notorious for frequent near-gale conditions of 30 knots (nautical miles per hour) of wind. Lows frequently develop between New Zealand and the trade-wind belt. After such poundings, many cruisers often lose their tolerance for further ocean passage making.

Wendy Hinman in *Tightwads on the Loose: A Seven Year Pacific Odyssey* sums up many cruisers' experiences, "The good news about our passage to Fiji [from New Zealand] was that we arrived safely; the bad news was that we had to live through it." She described 25-to-40 knot winds and 15-foot seas on the 11-day passage, acknowledging that their trip would have been much more pleasant had they sailed downwind to New Caledonia instead of upwind to Fiji.

Round trips can be appealing. It gives one a chance to stop at new places on the way back. Returning to familiar territory can be comforting. It just does not get you around the world. Every day spent backtracking is a day the cruiser will never have again. Eventually, life will intervene in terms of health, money, family, *et cetera* and put an end to the cruise.

I found that after two weeks in a particular port I started feeling like a commuter. The daily grind of the dinghy replaces the daily grind of the commute in the car. To a lesser extent, sailing over familiar seas can feel like an extended commute. At some point, we advance or stagnate.

The grind of sailing back and forth between Australia and other South Pacific destinations came through in Martin Lane-Smith's later *Podcastaway* podcast episodes. He spent several cyclone seasons on a mooring in Bundaberg, Australia, commuting in the months outside of cylcone season to Vanuatu, the Solomon Islands, and Papua, New Guinea. These passages on his large sailing catamaran *Dos Gatos* were often rough with beam on seas at best. At worst, he and his wife faced headwinds. They also had to move the boat outside of Australia each season to satisfy customs and immigration constraints.

After about four seasons of this, he and his wife sold the boat. They bought an RV to explore Australia. Nevertheless, after four years, it became hard to play tourist. Their family was half-way across the world.

They could have been in their home port after four years, but instead they had to see one more great dive site, which was not down wind. They ended up being fed up with life on a mooring. They listed their boat. Mr. Lane-Smith even says that they would be interested in living on a boat part-time in the Caribbean. After 11 years, they had enough of full-time cruising. My analysis of the *Latitude 38* data suggests that 88 percent of circumnavigations will take less than eleven years.

According to Jimmy Cornell, the numbers of boats continuing on a circumnavigation nearly halves after Australia. Thus, it seems that Martin Lane-Smith's experiences were not at all unusual. Indeed, Mr. Cornell quotes Tom Walker, "'Many world cruisers become caught in the South Pacific gyre. This is a vast imaginary current which sweeps cruisers north from New Zealand and Australia to the islands for the austral winter. It sweeps them south again for the cyclone season. Some cruisers become caught in the gyre for many years.'" [xi]

The cruisers caught in the "gyre" have to repeatedly cross one of the most notorious stretches of ocean, the Tasman Sea, which separates the islands nations of Vanautu and Fiji from New Zealand and Australia. A better solution is to not rush across the Pacific Ocean in an entire season. Haul out the boat in Raiatea. Fly back to your home, job, family, or do some land travelling, and then return to the South Pacific and sail for Tonga and Fiji the next season. Haul out the boat in Fiji. By repeating this process, you can avoid the round trips in stormy seas to and from Australia and New Zealand.

5. Comfort in the Off-Season

All the land based conveniences that the circumnavigator does without during the cruising season are much greater chores when the boat stops moving during typhoon season. Without new places to explore, the voyage stops being an adventure, and the hardships of boat life

41

start to grate on a full-time circumnavigator. In contrast, a part-time circumnavigator can limit her time to only when the adventure is ongoing and new ports are being discovered. When you are moving and exploring, the modern conveniences are not as important. In contrast, the discomforts of boat life have few redeeming qualities when the boat is idle during cyclone season.

You can get your fix of the modern conveniences by plane much easier than moving the boat back and forth from the less developed to the developed world. Upon arriving in New Zealand after months in the tropics, one circumnavigator wrote that he was starved for full-service grocery stores. Getting one's fix of modern life is just a plane flight away. Instead of sailing to New Zealand, he could have flown there or to his home country of the United States.

The smallest apartment is more comfortable than a 60-foot yacht parked in a marina, with its anchor down, or swinging from a mooring. Regardless of the size of your boat, you will find more comfortable shore-based lodgings out of season that cost less than keeping your boat safe and climate controlled with all its multitude of systems working.

The first shock that dirt dwellers experience when they buy a boat is how often stuff breaks down. The more systems there are on a boat, the more systems that can break down. If you are handy, you can fix stuff yourself, avoiding the hassle of hiring and managing workers and paying for their huge bills. Alternatively, you could go back to land-based accommodation and experience the relatively break-down-free existence for a few months while your boat has a dry storage berth in some exotic location.

The trade-wind circumnavigation traverses the tropics. Cyclone and hurricane seasons are in the summers. That means living on a boat out of the cruising season but in the tropical storm season is probably really hot. You could keep the shore power and generators working overtime to run the air conditioner (if you have such luxuries), but that is neither cheap nor trouble-free.

We were boiling in April in Key West after our cruise to the Bahamas. My wife and daughter were planning to fly out soon, so we could not just flee north to cooler latitudes. Unfortunately, our generator had a bad fuel filter and some watery gas. Our cooling lines for the air conditioner also had to be unclogged from seaweed. I only diagnosed and solved these problems after a week of trial and error and parts shopping. We could not afford the transient marina fees so we swung on a mooring in a well-protected but largely windless bay. I got the AC working and even bought a spare Honda generator. After Sophie and Janna flew out, I headed north just after the first named storm formed a few hundred miles to the east of Key West.

Unfortunately, full-time cruisers in the tropics cannot sail for higher latitudes once they have chosen their tropical storm season base. They are stuck until cruising season starts again. One full-time circumnavigator spoke of a mooring on a remote island that was near the equator and thus out of the cyclone belt, where he spent the South Pacific cyclone season. He spoke of boredom, petty rivalries, and insignificant slights both among the cruising boaters and the island residents. That circumnavigator avoided the round-trip problem with his typhoon season island, but that did not make for a great six months.

On a mooring or at anchor, the full-time circumnavigator in the off-season will likely have to transport fuel and water by dinghy. This is hot, hard work. Further, a watermaker may not save the full-time cruiser from schlepping water frequently. If she has a desalinator, it has a rigorous maintenance schedule. Further, it cannot be run if there is any oil, diesel, or gasoline floating around. The expensive reverse osmosis membrane will be destroyed if any petroleum products are in the water. If the cruiser needs a new membrane, she will have to go through the ordeal and expense of ordering parts in paradise. For all these reasons, running a watermaker in a crowded mooring field or dirty harbor is a bad idea. If you can't use a high-capacity watermaker, luxurious showers are probably not in the cards. Even the best boat shower is one-tenth as good as a shore based-shower.

Laundry is also a hassle. Some sailors wash laundry out of a bucket of salt water and rinse with fresh water stores. A full-time circumnavigator might find an expensive marina with laundry. (This is doubtful in many locations.) She also may find a place with laundry machines, but it will often be a long dinghy ride and a hike to get to it. A rare boat has a big enough a generator and a watermaker to run a washing machine. On top of that, all these interdependent systems are likely to break down. There is always the bucket method when either the watermaker, the generator, or the washing machine breaks down!

The most comfortable thing is to leave the boat for at least the six months during typhoon or hurricane season. In this way, the part-time cruiser will benefit from climate control, easy transportation, and improved diet and hygiene if they leave the boat for at least six months. The part-time circumnavigator can visit doctors and dentists covered by standard (domestic) health insurance. If they want to, a part-time circumnavigator can also earn money in their home country.

6.   Part-Time Cruising and Money

Part-time cruising is very common even for people who have "quit their jobs to live on a boat." The seasons often necessitate part-time cruising even if money concerns do not. Martin Lane-Smith's early part-time cruising from 2001 to 2005 did not seem to be driven by money. He and his partner were retired, but north Atlantic hurricane season encouraged the couple to move off their boat for about five months of the year while they explored the Bahamas and the Caribbean. He explains in his podcast:

"Initially, I looked at cruising as a sort of excursion in the sense that I viewed myself as living in California and going on six-month cruises on Dos Gatos. And then I would be back in California for the summer five months or so and then the month in Florida to get the boat ready and then go off for another cruise for six months. And I tend to think of it that way. For a couple of years, I still kept an apartment, Magic Flute [a Norsea 27' sailboat], and two vehicles in California; and I gradually shed those over the years because I really did not get enough time to mess with them. Now I still have one vehicle there (the Jeep Wrangler), but I have everything else in a storage unit. I have no other ties to the area. In particular, when we moved to Trinidad for hurricane season, the center of gravity shifted, and I tended to think of myself as living on the boat year round and then taking a two-month excursion back to California to take care of business. So I saw myself as boat centric. Whereas, prior to that I saw myself as living in California."

Cruising part-time can ease the transition from one's ties to one's home, cars, and other belongings.

Money also pushes many younger cruisers to cruise part-time. As I argued earlier, being stuck in port is not very rewarding. Earning money, keeping one's job market skills fresh, and refilling the "cruising kitty" (the savings to fund several months more travels) drives many younger cruisers to leave the boat or suspend the cruise.

Lin and Larry Pardey essentially suspended their cruising on their 24-foot sailboat *Seraffyn* so Larry could work at a boat yard in Virginia or as a sail maker's assistant in England. Prior to coming to Virginia, they spent a lot of time working in Miami to earn money. Work visas are often hard to come by. Thus, working cruisers will often have to return to their home country to get a job. Since it is much easier to fly back than move the boat to their home country, cruisers today can leave their boats to continue working.

Quitting one's job to live on a boat may lead to a big pay cut when returning to the workforce on a per hour basis. Outside of the most highly in-demand careers and professions many modern workers do not have a well-defined set of skills. Thus, job searches may be prolonged. Cruisers may have to accept large pay cuts. Waiting tables in the off-season may not be appealing to many potential full-time cruisers, who contemplate quitting their current jobs to go cruising. A better option is to arrange for a few months of unpaid leave. There are many jobs in which being there every day is not essential. Employers often want to retain a reliable employee by negotiating a few months of unpaid leave. For example, employers manage maternity leaves all the time. They can manage a three-month, unpaid sabbatical.

Educators and students have two-to-three-month breaks. Those breaks are perfect for part-time cruises. This is especially true if those extended cruises don't involve round trips. Business owners may find it hard to sell their businesses, but they may be able to step away from being on site for a few months at a time. Professionals may be able to limit their availability to just six to 10 months of the year. A dentist can decide to only take appointments for six months of the year, especially if he is in a practice with several other dentists. A medical doctor could seek out *locum tenens* for six months of the year, filling in for other absent doctors. Consultants or computer scientists could take assignments for only part of the year.

Franz Amussen worked as financial advisor for many years. On his podcast entitled *Sailing in the Mediterranean*, he explains that he typically took two months off from his work in Salt Lake City, Utah to cruise on his 28-foot sailboat in the Mediterranean in the summer months, the high season in the Med. Mr. Amussen probably could have retired and lived on his boat full-time if he had wanted to. Since he did not, we might conclude that he enjoys his part-time cruising more. Cruising part-time allowed him to go back to his practice and home in Utah.

7.   Exit Plan

A couple who quits their jobs and sells their home, and most of their worldly possessions has to start over when they return home — even if they decide the cruise is not for them after a few months or a year. This is very common according to *Get Her on Board* author Nick O'Kelly.

I crewed on a delivery trip where the beautiful, new, fully-loaded sailboat was supposed to be cruising the Bahamas and eastern Caribbean that season. Instead, after a few weeks in the boat, the couple decided cruising over the horizon was not for them. They flew back home to New Jersey and hired a skipper to sail their boat back from south Florida. Thus, they shelled out thousands of dollars to have somebody else sail their brand new world cruising boat, which they may now never take outside of the U.S.

At least they had a home to get back to. The stories are legion of one member of the couple, usually the female in the partnership, calling a very premature end to a long dreamed of cruise. With a two-to-six-month leave of absence from your job, it is no big deal to decide that circumnavigating is not for you. Just go back to your job and home and hire a skipper to sail your boat to a good place to sell it. Sure you lost some wages and may lose some money on the boat, but you can easily slide back into your old life. That is not necessarily the case if you sold your house and quit your jobs or sold your business. You may or may not get your old job back at your same salary or at all. Starting a new business is never easy.

In *Breaking Seas*, Glenn Damato realized that he does not like the cruising life after sailing his sailboat from San Francisco to Cabo San Lucas, Mexico. He was in a deep depression in a foreign port until he was able to win his old job back. Not all potential full-time circumnavigators will find such a happy ending, and some may never regain the earnings and status of their old employment. Dissatisfaction with the cruise is not the only reason why would be circumnavigations are aborted. Life events that often postpone leaving the dock can delay or end to a cruise. Health issues and family emergencies can come at any time. If the cruiser still has her old life to come back to, these problems may be more manageable. Most Americans have health care tied to their employers. If they permanently leave their jobs, they may be unable to pay for any serious health problems. Illness is one of the biggest causes of bankruptcy in the United States.

In the book, *Erisko Sails West: A Year in Panama*, Connie McBride tells of the difficulty of getting back surgery for her husband Dave after he ruptured a disk on their cruise, hauling heavy jerry cans. With no jobs to come back to and a non-working engine on their 34-foot sailboat, they had to struggle to get Dave McBride the medical care that he needed.

8.   Kids and School

For parents with children, part-time cruising may also make sense. Certainly, many families have successfully homeschooled their children while cruising full-time. Nevertheless, public or even private schools are a great service to parents. Educating a child or children of several different ages can easily become a full-time job. Many parents will not want to become both educators and cruisers. The educational duties may fall to one parent, marring her cruise since she has to play teacher while her husband plays sailor. If the family only cruises during the summer months, they can take advantage of the services of formal schooling. Summer cruising allows both parents to participate in the fun of sailing and cruising more equally.

Observing my own daughter, I have found that the peer pressure of a large group lesson can be much more effective in keeping her focused on the new material than one-on-one instruction.

It is often hard to find other boats with similarly aged children. On our Bahamas cruise, we only found one place where Sophie could find other playmates. That was in the large cruising destination of George Town, Exuma, where several hundred boats gather during the winter and spring. Less popular cruising destinations and marinas often lacked one other boat with children.

Wendy Hinman in her book *Tightwads on the Loose* wrote that her husband rarely saw any children during his family's circumnavigation. (He did OK in school. He went to MIT as an undergrad!) Nevertheless, most parents would prefer that their kids have frequent interactions with similarly aged children. Doina Cornell's family circumnavigated the globe while she was seven to 13. She told her story in her book *Child of the Sea*. (Her father was Jimmy Cornell mentioned earlier.) She and her brother had rocky starts to school when her family's seven-year circumnavigation ended.

Even experienced homeschooling parents will occasionally prefer to have their children attend school. Dave and JaJa Martin wrote *Into the Light: A Family's Epic Journey* about their trip to the Spitsbergen in the Arctic Circle in a 33-foot sailboat with their three children. The Martins completed a seven-year, trade-wind circumnavigation in a 25-foot boat in 1995 before embarking on the cruise to the Artic in the 33 foot sailboat, *Driver*. Despite homeschooling their children for many years, they enrolled some of their children in school in Norway for part of the 11,000-mile cruise.

Homeschooling is great, but it's not for everyone. On our cruise, I was always busy fixing stuff that broke, route planning, or hauling stuff in the dinghy. That left little time for me to give eight hours of pre-schooling curriculum to Sophie. Janna went to eight years of college and completed six years of residency and fellowship to practice medicine in pediatric endocrinology. She is not trained in early childhood education, elementary education, history, music, math, or science for elementary, middle, or secondary school. If she is going to put in a full day of work, she would rather work in her field of training than homeschool. I feel the same way.

I bet a lot of potential cruisers make the same decision and do not cruise while their kids are in school. Many would-be cruisers wait until their kids graduate from high school. The option that I advocate involves cruising during the summer breaks. A part-time circumnavigation can be done during summer breaks if the children attend school in the Northern Hemisphere.

My parents teach kindergarten and high school English. There are lots of trained certified teachers on land working for a pittance compared to similarly educated dirt dwellers. If you homeschool on a boat, you give up that free public education or low-cost private school for your kids. If someone makes $100,000 a year in her job and gives it up to homeschool, replacing free or say $10,000-per-year, private education, that is a bad financial decision. The only reason to make that financial sacrifice would be because you love homeschooling.

Cruising with kids is rare. In the 2015 George Town cruiser's regatta, only about six percent of boats were "kid boats". In the West Coast circumnavigator list, only eight percent of boats were "kid boats" according to my estimates. (I defined a "kid boat" as a boat with three or more people sharing the same last name.)

I suspect that most people that love sailing and cruising don't necessarily love homeschooling. For that reason, many people balk from cruising while the kids are still in school. This may be one reason why most "full-time" cruisers postpone full-time cruising until after the kids are out of the house. Wanting to be a sailor is not synonymous with wanting to be your kids' teacher. For now, we would rather our daughter, Sophie, has access to children her age during the school year and outsource the educational services to highly trained teachers.

9.   Breakdowns and Parts

A smart world cruiser has lots of spares. Nevertheless, we rarely think of everything. Besides, if you have a boat big enough to store all your spares, it would need to be twice as big as the boat you want to sail in! In short, you will have breakdowns. You will run out of consumables like filters before you finish your around-the-world cruise. That means you will have to deal with international shipping and waiting in port for parts. Both things are likely to be worse than a colonoscopy.

I know you think FedEx can ship overnight anywhere in the world. It is not true. Even if you don't mind paying $250 for shipping and $150 for customs duties on a $100 pump, it is impossible to ship it to most places where your boat will be.

That means you have to spend weeks of your time in paradise in expensive, dirty outposts such as Suva, Nassau, or Papeete, bleeding cash and time. You will want to hike the waterfalls, lie on the pristine beaches, and snorkel the unspoiled reefs. Who wants to frequent the Tahiti McDonalds!

The international logistics companies are illogical. I learned this lesson the hard way. They are only good at collecting your money. They are awful at shipping stuff when you leave the land of five-digit zip codes and freeways in your wake. I was 50 miles from Miami while on the island of North Bimini in the Bahamas, but there was only one international shipping company that shipped there. It lost the package sent to me and the package that I sent. Their customer service line in the Bahamas never picked up the phone and there was only an 800 number good for the U.S. on the web. They used outside contractors who don't give tracking updates. Two-day shipping turned into a week.

I did get my package thanks to the CEO of DHL Americas. If you are having trouble calling or corresponding with the top executives at FedEx, DHL, or UPS, you are not alone. Don't think they can bail you out in the islands. If the Bahamas is too remote, think what Vanautu will be like.

Even if the shipping companies do their jobs, the packages can be held up by customs in unknown locations for unknown reasons. Sorting this out will not only be expensive, but also it will be a mystery worthy of a novel. It will be a mystery you don't want to act out!

What is the only "reliable" way to bring back hard-to-get consumables or parts? Bring them in your luggage. That is right. You can trust the airlines more than FedEx. The odds that your luggage is a day late is less than 5 percent. The odds that your international package will be late or lost in the islands is 80 percent. You say, "Plane tickets are expensive." Bingo! You are correct. Nevertheless, if you are flying anyway, then your plane flight for parts is free.

On average, a part-time cruiser will be going back to her job, business, or home in the developed world in three months or less. Thus, resupply can be done via luggage. Sure, you may be stopped by customs and have to pay a fee. My wife did when she brought me a windlass and pump in her luggage on the flight to Nassau. That was infinitely better than the package being held by customs. My wife was delayed 20 minutes instead of our cruise being delayed weeks, waiting for parts to arrive.

If part of your crew is joining you midway through that season's travel, that is all the better. You can get needed parts or supplies that you forgot in that new crew member's luggage. This technique is not new and was mentioned in Erskine Childers' great sailing novel, *The Riddle of the Sands*. When your season's cruise is shorter, part-time versus full-time, then getting parts by plane flight is more feasible because you are more often flying back and forth to the boat.

10. Conclusion

There are widespread misconceptions by dreamy sailors about how one must go about a circumnavigation. Even "full-time" circumnavigations are part-time cruises. You don't need to sell every worldly possession that does not fit in a boat and quit your job or business. All you need to start a circumnavigation by sailboat is to carve out a few months each year to keep the boat moving forward.

The key is moving forward. You don't graduate from college by taking every course in the catalog. You take the courses required for your degree. Likewise, a circumnavigation does not visit every port in the globe. It is moving in a line around the world until you cross your outbound track. If you avoid the cruising season circle by hauling out your boat or tying it up at a safe marina, you can complete the circumnavigation challenge with far fewer sea miles under your keel.

The more round trips you avoid, the more likely it is that your crew and your bank account will not tire of the quest.

Part-time circumnavigators do not need to upend their careers or businesses which were built over several years. A couple does not have to pull their kids out of school or wait until they are grown. They will spend less time in dirty foreign ports waiting for parts than "full-time" cruisers. Many people's dreams of a circumnavigation have been crushed by the full-time circumnavigation fallacy. They had to wait until they retired. They had to wait until the kids were grown. They had to wait until they had enough money to fund many years of not working. I hope many readers throw off these misconceptions and start the cruise of their dreams.

At the time of writing, I don't know if my *Slow Boat* will ever make it around the world. I don't know if it will even make it to Panama. Nevertheless, I would rather have the circumnavigation in progress or ahead of me than in the rear view mirror. I would rather be preparing for a leg of the journey in a few months than saying, "Someday I'll do it when the time is right." The right time never comes. Get the boat, sail it, prepare, learn to maintain it, try some shorter cruises, get some offshore experience, choose a good weather window, and then just go. I hope that you complete your part-time circumnavigation even if I never do.

If you want to know more about future books and my family's travels, get free chapters or books, boat repair tips, and news of discounts, subscribe to my free newsletter at www.slowboatsailing.com. If you got to the end of this book, do a good deed that will help your fellow sailors by writing a review on Amazon. I hope you have fair winds and following seas.

Acknowledgements

A debt is owed to my wife, Janna, who provides encouragement with my writing and tries to ignore my mistakes on the water. I am also grateful to Beth M. Anderson for volunteering to proofread. Any errors here are my own.

I want to thank our sponsors who took a chance on an unknown author. On our next big cruise, our boat will be carrying a four-man, Revere Survival Offshore Commander 2.0, life raft. We will have the best sea anchor on the market, the Fiorentino Para-Anchor. In addition, we will have a Mantus anchor on our bow roller. There are links to all of their great products at www.slowboatsailing.com.

About the Author

photo by Janna Wilson, Linus and Sophie Wilson in S/V Contango in the Bahamas

Linus Wilson's first book, *Slow Boat to the Bahamas*, was a #1 bestseller in Bahamas travel guides and Kindle sailing narratives on Amazon. It is a funny look at getting the sailing bug and sailing to the Bahamas from New Orleans in 2015.

Linus Wilson has been published in *Good Old Boat*, *Cruising Outpost*, and *Southwinds* magazines. The author earned a doctorate in financial economics from Oxford University in England. On the dirt, he is an associate professor of finance at the University of Louisiana. He is married with one child, Sophie, above.

His family sails a 31-foot Island Packet, *S/V Contango*, which is better known as the *Slow Boat*. He jogs because he likes to sometimes travel faster than five knots.

To join the adventure, move towards the cruise of your dreams, and get news of free books subscribe to his free newsletter at www.slowboatsailing.com.

---

i Alan Arnette, February 14, 2014, "Everest by the Numbers: The Latest Summit Stats," accessed online on September 9, 2015, at http://www.alanarnette.com/blog/2014/02/20/everes t-numbers-latest-summit-stats/.

ii Mark Jenkins, June 2013, "Maxed Out on Everest," *National Geographic*, accessed online on September 11, 2015, http://ngm.nationalgeographic.com/2013/06/125-everest-maxed-out/jenkins-text. This article says that from 1953 to 2012, there have been 19,121 people who have climbed above base camp, and 6209 have

summited. Alan Borgna Brunner, "Everest Almanac: Mortals on Mount Olympus
A history of climbing Mount Everest," accessed online on September 11, 2015,
http://www.infoplease.com/spot/everest2.html says that 13 died prior to the first ascent in 1953. Alan Arnette, February 11, 2013, "Everest 2013: Has Everest Become More Dangerous?" accessed online on September 11, 2015,
http://www.alanarnette.com/blog/2013/02/11/everest-2013-has-everest-become-more-dangerous/ says from 1924 (the first summit attempts) to 2012, there were 232 deaths. Combining those three sources 219 have died since 1953 on 19,121 attempts above base camp, or a little over 1.1%.
[iii]

http://news.nationalgeographic.com/2015/05/150513-everest-climbing-nepal-earthquake-avalanche-sherpas/.
[iv] Jimmy Cornell, November 22, 2012, *Cornell's Survey of Global Cruising Yacht Movements*, accessed online on September 11, 2015, at
http://cornellsailing.com/de/2012/11/cornells-survey-of-global-cruising-yacht-movements/
[v] I want to thank Professor Paul Miller who pointed me in the right direction for these sources, but he is not responsible for any errors here. Paul H. Miller, March 27-28, 2004 "Risk Management in Sailing," (PowerPoint presentation), U.S. Naval Academy, Naval Architecture Program, Safety at Sea Seminar, accessed online on September 9, 2015, at
http://www.usna.edu/Users/naome/phmiller/_files/documents/publications/phmSAS04.ppt.
[vi] Statistics on deaths in sailboats and dinghies are from U.S. Coast Guard (USCG), "Recreational Boating Statistics 2011." Statistics on average hours spent in sailboats and dinghies (which is referred to as

"Row/Inflatable/Other Boat" by the USCG) are from U.S. Coast Guard, "2011 National Recreational Boating Survey."

[vii] The 965.5 hours per year and the 98 percent participation rate in automobiles comes from Diana Williams, 2009, "Arbitron National In Car Study, 2009 Edition," Arbitron. The 24,526 deaths in automobiles and the U.S. population numbers in 2009 are from the National Highway Traffic Safety Administration's (NHTSA's) Fatality Analysis Reporting Encyclopedia.

[viii] http://www.mounteverest.net/expguide/route.htm accessed online on September 13, 2015.

[ix] October 2, 2003, "CHO OYU 'Killer Mountains' - an ExplorersWeb series" accessed online on September 9, 2015, http://www.mounteverest.net/story/CHOOYUKiller MountainsanExplorersWebseriesOct22003.shtml.

[x] Martin Lane-Smith, November 5, 2007, "23: Fiji to New Caledonia," *Podcastaway*, podcast downloaded September 17, 2015.

[xi] Jimmy Cornell, November 22, 2012, *Ibid*.

71

15258715R00041

Printed in Great Britain
by Amazon